Enid Blyton

BIBLE STORIES

The Little Boy Jesus

ILLUSTRATED BY STEPHANIE McFETRIDGE BRITT

First published in 1996 by Candle
Books. Distributed by SP Trust Ltd,
Triangle Business Park, Wendover
Road, Aylesbury, Bucks HP22 5BL,
England

ISBN 1 85985 103 7

Designed and created by
Three's Company,
5 Dryden Street,
London WC2E 9NW

Illustrations by Stephanie
McFetridge Britt

Worldwide co-edition organised and
produced by
Angus Hudson Ltd,
Concorde House,
Grenville Place,
London NW7 3SA
Phone +44 181 959 3668
Fax +44 181 959 3678

Printed in Singapore

The Little Boy Jesus

When Jesus was a baby, his mother and father had to take him away from Bethlehem, where he was born, because the wicked King Herod had told his soldiers to kill all the boy babies there.

They fled away with him, and they did not come back to their own country until an angel told them it was safe to do so.

'Arise,' said the angel, 'and go back to your own land; for the king is dead who wanted to kill your child.'

So Mary and Joseph packed all their things, saddled their little donkey, and set off back to their own land.

'We will go to the town of Nazareth,' said Joseph. 'Our friends are there. We shall be happy in that place.'

5

And so one day they arrived at Nazareth, set high up on the green hillside.

'Now we are home again,' said Mary, gladly. 'See how the little white houses shine in the sun. We will have one of those to live in, Joseph, and our little Jesus shall grow up here and learn to help you in your workshop.'

So Jesus grew up in one of the little white houses on the hillside. In this little house Joseph set up his carpenter's shop. Mary and Jesus liked to hear all the hammering and sawing. Jesus often went into the shop and watched his father. He sometimes lifted a heavy hammer and played with the nails.

'One day I will help you,' he told Joseph. 'I shall be a carpenter too.'

9

Jesus did all the things that the other children of Nazareth did. He went to fetch water from the well in the old stone pitcher. He wandered over the hillside too, and picked flowers for his mother. He talked with the shepherds, and heard their tales. He played with the lambs, listened to the birds singing, and watched the sower sowing his seed in the fields.

His mother told him many stories. He knew the stories of Noah and his ark and Daniel in the lions' den. Mary taught him to obey God's commands, and to pray to him each day. Jesus listened eagerly, and learned everything his mother could tell him.

When he was old enough Jesus went to school. He had to learn his lessons and learn the law of God too.

The law of God had been written down by Jewish teachers. They had filled books full of tiny laws as well as big ones. The tiny laws told people exactly how they should wash a plate, and arrange their clothes, and things like that. When Jesus saw that the people sometimes thought more of doing these small things correctly than they did of big things such as being kind and generous to one another, he was puzzled.

'Surely it is better to be like old Sarah, who lives down the hill and is always kind to everyone in trouble, though she forgets the little commands, than it is to be like James, who never forgets the little things, but is unjust and unkind all the time,' thought Jesus.

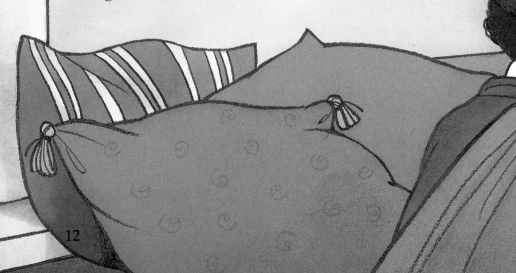

Twelve Years Old

Once each year the Jewish people kept a great feast, or holiday. They liked to go to Jerusalem, where their beautiful Temple stood. Joseph and Mary loved to go too.

'What do you do when you go there?' asked Jesus.

'There are meetings and services,' said Mary. 'And we meet many people, and see old friends. It is an exciting and happy time. When you are twelve we will take you with us, Jesus.'

So, when he was twelve years old, his mother kept her promise. 'You can come with us,' she said. 'You are a big boy now – you have learned the law of God, and it is time that you went to the Temple with us. You must promise to keep the law, you know.'

It was very exciting to think of such a long journey. Jesus had heard so much of Jerusalem and the Temple. Now he was really going to see it.

The great day came and Joseph and Mary were ready to go. Joseph shut the door of the little house, and smiled to see Jesus' excited face.

Other children were going too. They ran to join Jesus.

'Walk with us!' they cried. 'Come along!'

It was a lovely journey over the hills and plains to Jerusalem.

Each day was exciting – and the nights even more exciting! For then they lit camp fires, cooked meals, and sang old songs and hymns.

Then at last they came to Jerusalem, and went to the Holy Temple. Jesus stood and looked at the beautiful building.

'That is the house of God, my Heavenly Father,' he thought. 'I am going to his house.'

Jesus was taken into the Temple. God felt very near to him there.

He was taken before the wise men of the Temple, and they made him a follower of the Law.

'Now you must count yourself grown-up,' said the wise men. 'You must keep all God's laws.'

And then the great feast was over. It was time to go home.

'How lovely it has been to meet all our old friends again!' said Mary. 'And how nice it will be to be back home again in our own little house!'

Mary did not see Jesus all that day. She wondered where he was. Perhaps he was with the other boys.

'He's sure to come and look for us when we camp tonight,' she thought. But the night came, and there was no Jesus.

'We must look for him, Joseph,' said Mary, anxiously. 'Go and ask the other boys if they know where he is.'

'No,' said the boys. 'We haven't seen him at all.'
Nobody had seen him since they had left
Jerusalem. Mary and Joseph were very worried.

'We will go back to Jerusalem,' said Joseph. So
back they went. But still they could not find Jesus.

For three days they went up and down the
streets, asking everyone they met the same
question. 'Have you seen our boy, Jesus?'

'There is only one place left to look,' said Mary
at last. 'And that is the Temple itself. He loved the
Temple, Joseph. Perhaps he has gone back there.'

23

They went to look and there they found Jesus.
He had been in the Temple all the time

He had found the wise men, the ones who knew
more about the Jewish law than anyone in the
land. He had asked them questions – questions
they did not know how to answer! They were
amazed at this young boy who knew so much
about the law of God

They kept him there hour after hour, asking him
questions too. Jesus forgot everything except that
now at last he was finding out things he needed to
know. He felt very close to God in the Temple.

Here, in the Temple, he belonged to God, more
than he belonged to Joseph and Mary.

And then he suddenly saw his parents nearby, looking at him with anxious, troubled eyes! Mary went to him, weeping with joy.

'Son!' she said. 'Why have you behaved like this? Your father and I have been looking for you everywhere. We have been so worried.'

Jesus was surprised. 'But did you not guess where I would be?' he said. 'I had to come to my Father's house, and learn the things I should know.'

He went home with Mary and Joseph. He became their young son once more, and obeyed them in all things.

He settled down again in Nazareth helping
his father and mother, until he was a man.
But he often thought over all the
things he had
learned in
the Temple.